Bare Feet
to
High Heels

You are a beautiful person!

_____

Bare Feet

to
High Heels

You don't have to be
a beauty queen to be
a beautiful person

Jane Jenkins Herlong

Bare Feet to High Heels
You don't have to be a beauty queen to be a beautiful person

Jane Jenkins Herlong

Contact information:
Jane Jenkins Herlong
65 Bouknight Road
Johnston, SC 29832

Phone: 803-275-3388
Fax: 803-275-2766
jane@janeherlong.com
http://www.janeherlong.com

Cover design and layout: Ad Graphics, Inc., Tulsa, OK
Printed in the United States of America

ISBN: 0-9711467-0-5

DEDICATION

This book is dedicated to my sweet,
supportive husband, Thomas
and my precious children,
Thomas Holmes Herlong, Jr.
and Eleanor Caroline Herlong.

CONTENTS

Introduction

I grew up watching the Miss America Pageant. Like many folks I believe Miss America is a symbol of the great American dream. Most of us are fascinated with the idea of "small town girl-next-door becomes overnight celeb."

Every second weekend in September you will find me plastered to the television watching the pageant. My freshman year in college I was so glued to the television I plugged the wrong wire into the wrong appliance and almost burned down my dormitory!

Maybe a fire was lit under me since, only a few years later, I was one of 50 women who walked up to the mic at Convention Center in Atlantic City, New Jersey, and introduced myself to gazillions of Americans. I just prayed that nobody barked or howled like I had done to contestants over the years!

Did I win Miss America? No. But, did I win? YES. I was given a wonderful gift—the chance to be pulled, poked, stretched, and sprayed. Yes, even sprayed. Twice a week I was wrapped in gauze and sprayed with this pink stuff to try to reduce the size of my legs. Like my mother always said, "Colonel Sanders could make a mint off of your thighs." All in the line of duty for beauty.

Honorary Miss Americas

- Cinderella
- Scarlet O'Hara
- Lucille Ball
- Richard Simmons
- Mother Teresa
- Barbara Bush
- Oprah

This book will make you laugh and give a few "rhinestones" to help you sparkle and shine without using an ounce of firm grip on your bottom, surgical tape on your top or Vaseline on your teeth.

Cinderella: The Ultimate Miss America

Cinderella. She thought pleasant thoughts and sang with her little friends. She was not lazy at all. She did her chores while her no-good, lazy stepsisters (skinny girlfriends) lounged around expecting to be waited on. Enter the "fat girlfriend" (fairy godmother) who tells her truths and helps create the killer gown complete with rules and transportation to the ball.

Cinderella walked into the dance and just "was." She did not know or care for that matter that the prince was THE PRINCE. She just danced, laughed, and had fun. She had him at "hello." Then the clincher—she disappeared without giving phone number, address, nothing. The wise Fairy Godmother knew that if she disappeared into the night, he would climb Mount Everest to find her. The queen's rule—always leave them wanting more. We all know the rest of the story.

You may be thinking, "Okay, Jane, it works great for fairytales BUT how about in the real world???? Huh????" *My theory is you don't have to be a beauty queen or princess to be a beautiful person. Just be the best person you know you can be and the rest will follow.*

You are the magic wand. Start where you are and expand the good and work on the bad and the ugly. We all have good, bad and ugly somewhere in our person. Be honest and tackle all the stuff that needs work. Discipline gives birth to confidence, and when you have confidence in yourself…watch out!

Question: What is a mirror?
Answer: A beauty queen entertainment center.

Bless the Beast and the Beauty Queens

In the South we love to celebrate. Just pick a title and somewhere down the secondary roads of the rural South, there will be an event thought-up by folks who just want to party. This is the genesis of queens. If you want to have an event first you have to draw a crowd of people. What attracts folks? Purty girls.

I have been in a parade with the Kudzu Queen. That's what I said, "Kudzu." These are pesky green vines that grow out of control across our Southland. It's like Southern politicians—they hang around forever.

One of my favorite titles of all time is Miss "Pullit." This represents only the finest young ladies who have the insatiable desire to be the queen of the Tractor Pull Festival in Saluda County.

Some of our queens have had humble beginnings. Former Miss Universe, Shawn Weatherly, of South Carolina fame once reigned our state as "Miss Fresh Fruit and Vegetable."

Yes, we have the titles...Miss Chitlin Strut, Queen of Catfish "Feastival" (they feast on catfish), Miss Railroad Days, Miss Frog Jump, Miss Okra and the Pork Queen only to highlight a few.

Through the years I have learned that queens come in many shapes, colors and sizes. From Miss Kudzu to Miss America, these women have been a part of a wonderful American tradition: competition. It is through competition that you learn about yourself and how to evolve into your best self. The key is don't be afraid to try!

I have seen many people enter competitions and not get as much as an "atta girl/guy." After the hoopla dies, the reward surfaces…..a personal win. There is victory in competition. YOU gotta find it!

"Good, better, best; never rest till 'good' be 'better' and 'better' best."

– Mother Goose

CHAPTER 1

Poise:
Walking with the Dead

Billy's Funeral Home

In the "minor league" pageants there are 4 categories on the judges' ballots: poise, smile, projection, and overall appearance. It doesn't take a genius to figure out that poise is smile, projection and overall appearance. In fact, poise is everything.

Poise can turn a "you-don't-have-a-chance, Honey" into a "where-did-she-come-from?" Amazing.

In our state there was one man who could help queens achieve perfect poise. I heard that his technique was the best in the South and to perfect took years of practice and discipline. I heard that he had so many winners he lost count. His accolades included the likes of "Miss Universe" to "Little Miss Saturday Afternoon at The Mall."

One would think his place of business would be located in one of those bridal/pageant shops that dot across our southern landscape. You would think that the owner wore a shade of bruised blue eye shadow and had high ceiling fans in case of big hair accidents. No, to receive a Ph.D. in poise, the queens lined up in procession to Billy's Funeral Home.

To say Billy was the master of the human body is an understatement. Dead or alive, he was good at his trade. Billy used his funeral home tricks to remedy pageant girl atrocities. He would boast about the big plug of wax he used to fill a hole in Ann Marie Smith's leg—an injury sustained from a childhood accident. And for a finishing touch, Billy pressed a paper towel over the area to give the wax a "porous look." He pioneered the fine and delicate art of wearing medical tape instead of underwear or "drawers" as they are more commonly known in the South.

Twice a week I would faithfully travel 180 miles to Sumter, South Carolina, dressed only in a leotard, high heels and a smile. All day I would do one thing: WALK. "Ankles together, drop-back, half turn to the right, half turn to the left, full turn, quarter turn, right stance, left stand, hesitation, line up......," Billy would command as we negotiated our "living" bodies between caskets, urns and "Jesus Called" telephone wreaths. Billy had two huge mirrors set up: one in the casket room and the other in the "grievin' family room." Of all the hours I spent walking, I'm sure I could have traveled to Atlantic City and back. There were only two rules: 1. When the doorbell rings, run and hide. 2. Always call before you come in case there is a dead body.

I would never eat before I went to see Billy because the first thing he would do is get out his trusty tape measure. He kept very strict records about your size. For lunch I would gnaw on hamster food while he ate a Big Jim Double Chili Cheeseburger and a large order of cheese fries. I think he would eat that stuff just to test my willpower.

It was particularly tough when Monta would walk with me. Monta—her name alone conjures an image of someone with perfect beauty. She was gorgeous and had a fabulous figure—nothing was "sto' bought." I was Miss Charleston and she was Miss Hickory. We would talk about being in the Miss America Pageant together. Billy was so proud when we both won our state titles.

Some of y'all may think Billy was on the "prissy" side. In touch with his feminine side he was but Billy was all man. He eventually opened a beauty queen boutique in the funeral home stocked with swimsuits, acrylic pumps, and beaded gowns. Yes, Billy was the master. He taught me volumes about how good bodies can look dead or alive. God love him.

I learned that poise commands respect. Poise speaks in a crowded room without opening your mouth.

Billy's bullets for walkin' queenly; purchase a full-length mirror and watch yourself walk. Filling your lungs with air will position your body in proper alignment. Gracefully swing your arms and let your fingertips brush your side. Cup your hands as if you are holding some loose pearls for a natural look. Then walk. Walk. And walk some more!

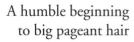

A humble beginning
to big pageant hair

People pay big bucks
for lips like these

Very 70's

CHAPTER 2

Be Real:
"Honey, Just Be Yourself"

My mother always told me, "Honey, just be yourself" and I took it to heart. Find pride in yourself and your roots.

"I bet if I run down there and tear that crown off her head, I'll get on the Johnny Carson Show."

– Delta Burke, Miss Florida, quipped as her
competitor was being crowned Miss America.

Hello, I Am Miss South Carolina!

"Jane, if you want to win Miss America, don't talk Southern and PLEASE don't throw in that Gullah!"

I practiced and practiced getting rid of my Southern accent! Can you believe it? I tried to hide it! Shame on me! I was not following my mother's advice. I knew better than to try to act like a generic beauty queen from nowhere. I soon discovered other contestants did the same thing.

"Hello, I am Miss South Carolina," I said in my new, perfect, UN-Southern brogue. It just rolled off of my tongue. Instead of hearing, "How-wah-yuh? I'm Miss New Yoooork."

The New York beauty queen answered, "Hello, I am Miss New York." Perfect. Sounded just like me.

"Hello, I am Miss South Carolina," I said again. This time I was introducing myself to Miss Texas. "Well, howdy, Girlfriend! How's yo' Momma and dem?" did not come out of her ruby-red, perfectly penciled, Texas lips. Instead the same ol', flawless response, "Hello, I am Miss Texas." Hmmmmmmmm.

Well, I'll be. Practically every contestant did the same thing I did. We lost ourselves.

Then it happened. Was I hearing things? Somewhere in that crowd of generic wannabes was a Southern accent as thick as pluff mud on low tide.

"Hey, Y'all! I'm so happy to be in this big ol' city. I'm from Choctaw County Mis'sippi! How y'all?" A hush fell over the room. We looked and stared at the brunette from Mississippi. "She will never win," commented one of the queens as she posed in her beauty queen stance. "Listen to that accent!"

One week later the newspaper headlines said it all:

Mississippi Beauty Wins Miss America!

Yeah, I learned a lesson......be who ya 'sposed to be!

Spanish Moss and Pluff Mud... Lowcountry Living

I love being from the Lowcountry of South Carolina. Most people agree; the South is a fascinating place.

A cousin of my husband's was transferred to South Carolina after living in Indiana for years. His friends all commented, "How are you going to stand living in the South? I mean there is no running water or electricity!" These friends were not trying to be funny; they actually believed this to be true! This family decided to have some fun with their friends back in Indiana. Their first Christmas in the South, they had a hilarious picture made into Christmas cards. They were all dressed in their "Sunday best" standing in front of an old, abandoned shack. The caption read, "We just love living in the South."

It is true that our ways in this part of the country are unique. Since I grew up outside of Charleston, I am a product of many unusual "Southernisms." For example, if you live south of Broad Street, you are known as an SOB. This is an honorable title, for only the finest "blue-bloods" live in this area of the Charleston peninsula.

We also take pride in being steeped in tradition. I read a joke in *The Post and Courier* to illustrate this point: How many Charlestonians does it take to change a light bulb? The answer is five, one to change the bulb and the other four to talk about how good the old one looked!

Southerners love to talk about their roots and what their families did before the "War of Northern Aggression." It is considered a "sin of the South" not to qualify your ancestry. The problem is only a select group is interested in who gave birth to whom, old money or new money, etc. Okay, so I'm one of them.

My family is from Johns Island. The Jenkins family takes pride in being known as "good island people." My grandfather, known as "Gumpa," always commented, "Thank Gawd they built that bridge." We needed to get on the other side of the Stono River to marry outside of the family.

Gumpa was such a character! One day Daddy drove him across the Cooper River Bridge (a good 2 miles expansion).

Gumpa was so afraid of crossing the bridge he wore a ski-belt! (For those of you who don't know what a ski-belt is, it is a lifejacket.)

As always, the people make the island special. I grew up with a network of relatives and African-American people who helped nurture and teach me an appreciation for their ways.

My family was blessed to have wonderful women help in our home who are an extension of my family. I have so many precious memories of Roseanne, Wilahmena and Tootsie. Tootsie still helps my mother and makes the best biscuits you ever put in "yo mout." She has been a part of my family for over forty years.

Tootsie and I love to laugh together. She is my "I Love Lucy" partner. Before I was old enough to attend school, I knew how the hands on the clock were positioned when it was ten o'clock in the morning. I would take her by the hand, park in front of the television, and for thirty minutes laugh at Lucy.

I Raise Dis Chile Sence She Been Five Munt Ol!

I love the language of Gullah. Gullah is the "Mother Tongue of the Sea Islands." This dialect is not necessarily spoken by a certain race of people. Gumpa spoke Gullah with unique eloquence.

Not too long ago, we went to pay our respects to a gentleman named Robbie, who passed away. Everyone loved Robbie since he was a very respected farmer on Johns Island. Tootsie asked me to go with her to the church to view the body. Knowing how scared Tootsie can be, I thought someone should tote her there.

We walked into the empty church filled with flowers and blue ribbons, Robbie's favorite colors. Just as Tootsie and I leaned over the casket, the smoke-alarm battery made that "low battery" sound. Tootsie screamed, jumped and grabbed me. She scared me so badly I grabbed her! We laughed buckets after we figured out what was going on! Tootsie exclaimed, "Gret Gawd, Jane, I sho thought Robbie was gwine git up out dat casket!"

Roseanne worked for us when Momma was expecting my brother. Momma began to have horrible labor pains. Roseanne, in her 'old school' way said, "Miss Eleanor, go quick an' git me duh hatchet and uh bobbie pin! Den go lie down on duh bed! I gwine put dat hatchet un'neath duh bed so it can cut duh pain! An dat bobbie pin gonna hold duh pain till that baby bon!" Momma told me that when you hurt you'll try just about anything.

Daddy came into the house to eat dinner, chuckling all the way to the table. "Boy, Lab sure put a cussin' on me today! He said, 'Mr. Benjamin, when you shet yo' eye fo the last time, I gwine tell dem peoples to bury you under eight feet deep! Dat way when Gabriel blow his horn, you be the last one up!'"

One of the best stories Daddy told was about taking our male cat to the veterinarian to be neutered. Daddy asked a farm worker named Lewis to hold the cat in his lap while Daddy drove. All the way to the veterinarian's office, Daddy heard Lewis lamenting, "Gret, Gawd, kitt'nee, I sho glad I ain't you!"

Johns Island Wisdom

Most Southern churin' have been "adviced" to death by our parents. When I was a child if a dark cloud suddenly came up, we knew what to do. First, put on your tennis shoes. Second, throw the cat outside (Momma said they attract lightning), don't look in a mirror or stand by a window. Don't even think about going into the bathroom or kitchen. And if you sit down, make sure whatever you are sitting on is not against a wall. Do these things or you will die.

Here are some more gems:

- Wear shoes in the winter since colds start in the sole of your feet.

- If a crab bites your toe it won't let go until it thunders.

- Wait an hour after you eat to swim or you will drown.

- Do not put down an open Co-cola at a party or someone will throw Marijuana in it.

- Do not drink out of a public water fountain; you will get AIDS.

This next piece of advice was given to my sister and me after we married.

- Take care of your man and do your "homework"; for every headache you have, there is a woman with an aspirin.

*Honey Is a Ho

This is my favorite story since my Mother was trying in her best way to give us girls advice about having good morals. Our lesson just happened to coincide with our dog, Honey, being "overheated."

Honey must have had a gazillion dogs following her around in our yard. "You see that!" Momma shouted as she looked out of the back door. "See how popular Honey is with all the dogs? I want you girls to remember how many friends Honey has now. But let me tell you in a few weeks, no one will be her friend! Soon she will be taking care of half-breed, yapping mutts. No fun trips to the beach with friends; no more going to the mall. I don't ever want you girls to let your morals go like Honey. I hope you have learned a lesson today."

Well, Honey all of a sudden was not popular and, yes, she did have a pre-me litter we call, "Heinz 57" breed. The saddest part is I decided to take the pre-me mongrels for a boat ride. Unfortunately they "passed" from the excitement of my motoring through the hairpin turns of Hut Creek.

We had Honey for several years and when she died, I was so upset I missed a day of school. I learned a lot from that bleached-blonde dog.

You Guys in the South Have Such an Accent!

The further up North I go, the more syllables I put in my words.

A friend of mine called the other day and asked, "Jane, why are Southern women so popular?" "I don't know!" I ex-

* Name was changed to protect the dog

23

claimed with great anticipation. "Because it takes y'all so long to say, Q——U——I——T!"

On a speaking engagement up Nahth (North), a Nahtherner asked me a rather unusual question, "Geez, if you and your husband were to get a divorce, would you still be considered brother and sister?"

Southern women don't sweat, we mist..................and then we glow.

Some officials at the Summer Olympics held in Atlanta were afraid that when the torch in the Olympic Stadium was lit that some good ol' boys from South Georgia were going to throw a hog up there and have a barbecue. You don't have an open flame in the South for nothing.

Jay Leno, host of *The Tonight Show*, quipped that then 92-year-old South Carolina Senator Strom Thurmond, head of the Senate Armed Services Committee, was considering re-opening some closed military facilities...beginning with Gettysburg.

"The people in Edgefield County love Senator Thurmond so much if he had died the day before his election we would have still voted for him." *The New York Times*, Suzy Holmes, Johnston, S.C.

I must comment on my friend Suzy and her hubby, Walker. At one of our church circle meetings, Suzie entertained the group speaking in her wonderful Southern drawl about how Walker celebrates Valentine's Day. "Now, Walker does not care much to celebrate the normal holiday, birth-day stuff that other people do. But, when it comes to Valentine's Day, he goes all out. Last year, he served me break-fast in bed with his delicious pancakes. Then he said he had a special treat for me outside. You know what he did? He wrote WALKER LOVES SUZIE with Round-Up weed killer in the field behind our house. You'd have to fly over it to get the full effect. He is so sweet."

Suzie also told me that Walker taught their children how to read using the *National Enquirer*. She said the sizes of the letters are so large that it helped them learn how to read faster. Their churin' may have learned about Elvis landing a space ship in Las Vegas but there must be something to Walker's reading technique. Their oldest child, Callie, has been given a scholarship to Harvard.

Speaking of Ivy League education...A smart Southern Belle was having a conversation with a good ol' boy. "Where ya goin' to college?" asked the good ol' boy? "Yale." Replied the Southern Belle.

"WHERE YA GOIN' TO COLLEGE?" he shouted!

When I travel to other parts of the country, people love to hear me speak "Southern." At a banquet a few years ago, after being asked repeatedly to talk, I noticed the waiters were serving lemon pie for dessert. I held up my hand and in my best Southern drawl said, "Why is my ha-nd like a piece of lem-on pie? Cause its got meringue (my ring) on it."

Yes, we take pride in the South...maybe at times too much.

My Cousin Earl shared a story about an overbearing Texan visiting Tennessee and bragging about how big everything is in his state. They saw a jackrabbit hop across the road and the Texan asked, "Hey, Man, what was that?" The Tennessean replied, "That is a rabbit." "Well," the Texan commented, "that is mighty small!"

Then they happened upon a goat grazing on a hillside. "What is that?" asked the Texan again. "Why, that is a goat." replied the Tennessean playing along with the Texan. "Well, I declare," said the Texan, "our Texas goats are three times the size of that critter!"

A few miles later, the Texan spotted a turtle slowly making its way across the highway. "Now what do you suppose that is?" quipped the Texan. Finally the Tennessean, in his monotone Southern, drawl muttered, "A tick."

If you are a real person,
you attract real people . . .

Thatgirlisdalin'

On a flight from St. Louis to Steamboat Springs, I had the chance to sit with a wonderful woman from another part of the universe—Staten Island. Her name is Nancy and we immediately hit it off.

We were wearing a black turtleneck, black jeans, and a colorful, wool parka. In her New York accent she exclaimed, "Luk at us! We heve on the same clothes!" That started a conversation that lasted a good two hours. She did not come up for air and was as cellophane as any person I have ever met.

The first thing she did was lean her head down and ask in her Staten Island accent, "Am I going bawld? I just came baack from the Caymans on a scuba diving trip. FABULOUS! Evah bin? The stingray suck squid from your hend. Did you know that they heve no teeth? They suck. I did nat want those things to suck my hend! Well, this guy put this squid on my hed and the stingray sucked my haiah! I thought I hed a Stealth bomma sitting on my hed! I hed a blest!

Do I look swollen? Eight years I gave thet man! Eight years!! He went through a mid-life, shaved his hed and bought a Harley. He went down to South Carolina and got with this piece of white tresh and broke my heart! Those Southern women are so treshy; they make me sick! Where did you say you were from?" I said, "Nebraska."

The postscript is that Nancy and I continued to communicate all year. She invited me to spend a few days with her in New York City before Christmas. I took my daughter Caroline and we had a blast! She is coming down South and I just may take her to the biker rally in Myrtle Beach. It just might rival the scenery in Time Square at 2 AM.

Hey, Sweet Thang!

Every time I hear the words, "Sweet Thing," I think of my pal, Red. One hot, July day in the little town of Gaffney at the South Carolina Peach Festival, I met Big Red.

It's right easy to catch a visual on this one…Big Red. First of all you know he is big and second, his hair color is a deep shade of Tang. With a name like his you can bet he is packaged "extra friendly."

I heard Red, not to be confused with "heard of," before I ever saw him. A blast from an "ooohgah" horn heralded his entrance down Main Street in Gaffney, South Carolina. Around the corner Red maneuvered his late-modeled, white Cadillac with blood-red, leather interior. Before I knew it, he was swinging queens around calling us all "sweet thang" and handing out packs of Big Red chewing gum and silver dollars.

Everyone was pretty much running for cover except me. He may have acted like a bulldog but to me Red was all "puppy."

We wrote each other several times and he sent me pictures of himself posing with Playboy bunnies at various Nascar events. We were both looking forward to seeing each other at the Miss Southern 500 Pageant.

Labor Day weekend arrived and all of us queens met in Darlington, South Carolina for the festival. The director of the pageant warned about this "pesky character" who loved beauty queens. I thought, "Well that takes care the entire male population—heterosexual and homosexual."

The director said, "His name is Red Robinson. Do not speak to him." What? Not sweet, innocent Red! No way was I going to avoid him!

Minutes later I heard Red wheeling his white Cadillac through the parade route trying to find me. I hopped down off my float and gave him a big ol' hug.

Fast forward with me, one year later. It is Saturday morning at The Greenville Memorial Auditorium. That night, a new Miss South Carolina would be crowned. We were all clueless about who was in the lead except for the preliminary winners.

My thoughts were interrupted with a shout of, "Miss Charleston, telephone!" I thought this was weird since they never let us receive calls. Answering the phone, I heard the familiar, "Hey, there, Sweet Thang!" It was Red!

"Well, darlin' I just talked to your chief judge. You see, me and him go way back. I told him you was a real sweet thang and he best pick you tonight to win. He told me you was gonna win and so I just wanted to be the first to congratulate our new Miss South Carolina! Bye, now!"

I dropped the phone.

Red was the last person I thought would know one of the judges. Did it really make a difference in my winning the pageant? Probably not. It just made me feel good knowing I treated him like my parents taught me. Actually, Red taught me a lesson. You never know who will cross your path in life. Just treat folks the same way you want to be treated regardless of who they are.

"The best portion of a good man's life, his little, nameless, unremembered acts of kindness and of love."

– William Wordsworth

BSBQH—(Big Southern beauty queen hair)

The BIG moment being crowned Miss South Carolina 1980

CHAPTER 3

Be Fake:
Trainers, Wonderbras,
Hydrobras, and Silicone
(Maybe I should say—know how to fake it.)

Four Hooks or Bust

Growing up can have its challenges and mine began the summer before I entered junior high. Sitting behind Becky Stuhr in summer school was my first indication that life is not fair. Through the cotton blouse, across her back I saw the wide lace band. In the center of her back connecting the beautiful undergarment was not one hook, not two hooks, but four of them! My thoughts were then directed to Ricky White, who sat behind me. He is probably laughing at my "bra": a cotton tee shirt with the little pink bow.

My quest for the 4-hook bra started when Momma took me to visit The Lingerie Lady at Belk's department store. Mrs. Jorden was her name, and she was the bra expert. I will never forget her "ruby-red" lips, ivory skin and coal-black hair. However, the most outstanding feature, (or should I say features) was her "full" figure. Reminds me of that old joke, why does Dolly Parton have such small feet? 'Cause nothing ever grows in the shade. Well, let's face it, Mrs. Jorden was qualified (maybe over-qualified) to sell bras.

I was somewhat excited about entering womanhood. I could not wait to repeat the adventure to my best friend, Leize. Hopefully this time I would not confuse the particulars. The last time I recounted the "little talk" Momma and I had, I told Leize that once a month women have to wear a Q-tip.

A feeling of wonder and excitement swept over me as we wound our way through racks and tables of bras and panties to find The Lingerie Lady. While Momma chatted with Mrs. Jorden, I stared longingly at the 4-hook bras. Momma then summoned me over for Mrs. Jorden to literally size me up. My excitement was changed to dismay after being ushered to the "trainers".....only one hook.

Why do they call these bras, "trainers"? What are you training them for, anyway? And why don't men have to wear "trainer" athletic supporters? Men seem to have more trouble than women keeping things in place. Just watch a baseball game.

Anyway, dejected, I was escorted to the dressing room to try on the "foundation garment." To make matters even worse, my mother was standing outside of the dressing room giving commands like a Drill Sergeant." Fall in!" she yelled. My response was, "What are you talking about? Fall into what?" There was nothing to put anywhere.

After a "hands-on" demonstration with The Lingerie Lady and much discussion, Mrs. Jorden suggested we go to the store next door. Red-faced, I walked away, knowing in my heart I was not yet ready to enter the world of 4-hook bras.

It just could not get any worse, but it did. The "next door" place was Woolworths, no dressing rooms, no privacy. In front of God and the world, I was fitted to the most pitiful excuse of a one-hook bra ever made. This thing did not even resemble a bra; it was more like two squares of fabric connected with a strip of cloth. I felt like I was wearing size, "Band-Aid."

These are the times that try an adolescent's soul . . . open showers at cheerleader camp. I don't think I took a shower the entire week at camp. I was so afraid that one of the girls was going to yell, "There is a boy in the shower!" when I stepped in wearing my birthday suit.

I did not like those blonde twins that stayed in my dorm. I'm sure they became head waitresses at Hooters. Although Thomas did tell me that he thought I could get a job working at Hooters.........washing dishes.

Floating Friends

I guess you are wondering how I made it all the way to The Miss America Pageant. I am not exactly 36-23-36. But there are these lovely little helpers that can give you the hour glass figure needed to compete.

You can fake it at Miss America but not in the Miss USA/ Miss Universe system. They actually have designated personnel that "check" your swimsuit and evening gown to make sure it is all you. Most men would pay to have that job.

However, there should be a warning attached to wearing such enhancers. DO NOT JUMP INTO A SWIMMING POOL OR JUMP OFF A DIVING BOARD WHILE US-ING. THIS CAN CAUSE EMBARRASSMENT. This is first hand info, believe me.

While on our Honeymoon, I decided to pack my Miss America swimsuit and, of course, my "accessories." After all, I was attached to them.

After getting the attention of all 85 honeymoon couples who were basking around the pool, I jumped into the water.

The look of horror on Thomas' face as I surfaced said it all. Panicked, he gestured for me to turn around. Yes, there they were like two jellyfish fish (or, should I say, foam fish) bobbing on the wake. My little cone-shaped friends were right behind me. They made it to the surface before me. You would think that moment of embarrassment would serve to teach a lesson on what not to do, but noooooooo, only minutes later it happened again.

Thomas over-heard this guy, who was also on his honeymoon, comment, "Man, I feel sorry for him."

Right after that I returned to Atlantic City for the Miss America Pageant and told the story to my good friend, Donnie Smith. He laughed so hard I thought I was going to have to drag him off Atlantic City Boulevard. I said, "Promise you won't tell ANYBODY that story!" He said, "Oh, Jane, you know me. I can keep a secret!" Within hours people from every state in the union burst out laughing when I walked by.

Sto' Bought or Real?

If you have ever been to Florida to witness a launch, the first thing you notice are the space shuttles sitting proudly straight up. This reminds me of watching swimsuit competition at Miss USA and Miss Universe (okay, I'll admit Miss America, too).

A new preliminary should be added to swimsuit called "Silicone or Blessed-of-God"? Be honest, we all try to guess. "Look at Miss California's!" All the women chant. Of course the men just grunt.

I know queens who have had silicone implants after their reign was over! They are the antique implants, too. One girl swore to me that every night she had to put a book on each one and rotate it ten minutes to the left and ten minutes to the right for the rest of her life! Can you imagine?

Now with the new and improved implants there is a massive selection: saline, soybean oil, water, and even "watch me grows."

I went for my first mammogram and asked questions about women who have implants. The technician told me with silicone you only get a 20 percent reading from the images. But the most eye-opening comment was 99 percent of the women with implants said it was their FIRST husband's idea.

If you think you must go "under the knife" to catch a man, I believe you're fishin' in the wrong pond.

Queen's rule: *you don't need those things to lasso the right kind of man.*

My husband told me that if I really wanted a "set" he would buy me some for Christmas. He said since they are sooooo expensive, I could have one implanted this year and the other next year.

———

Going to a Victoria Secret store is like a trip to the Barbie "dreamstore." It is an insult to have the clerk ask, "Now, what size bra do you wear?" To which I reply, "Honey, if I wanted a real bra I would go to Wal-Mart. I want to look like one of those babes in your window. I would prefer being asked, what size do you want to be?"

You know people are talking when someone anonymously mails you a coupon for a "Wonder Bra." Of course, I got in line at Victoria's Secret and bought the thing. I showed it to Thomas. He said, "I know why they call it a Wonder Bra. 'Cause I am wondering what you have stuffed in it."

Wonder Bras have these interesting little pads called "cookies." The more cookies you buy the bigger the batch (or breasts). My problem was that I kept losing my cookies! I would find them all over the house and had a fear of them falling out at the mall or grocery store. I frequently did a "cookie check" to make sure all was well.

That which I feared the most came upon me. I did my "check" and discovered I was missing some cookies! Furthermore, I had just been to Bi Lo and had visions of them lying on the floor right by the frozen green peas.

My mind raced as sounds of my 4-year old playing with his Little Tikes truck interrupted my thinking. "Beep, beep, beep." Holmes chanted, "Watch out! The truck is backing up!" I looked down at his cargo. In the back of his little, green truck were my cookies. They must have fallen out in the kitchen when I was putting up the groceries. Holmes was taking them for a ride.

Of course this is the same child who just recently saw a hydrobra in the store and proceeded to yell, "Momma, you really need this!" and held it up. I just kept walking and pretended he belonged to some other flat-chested woman.

It may amaze some that I did breast feed my children for the first year of their lives. I weaned Holmes when he "unlatched" from one side, looked up at me in precious baby innocence and said, in perfect English, "Cracker?"

My sister, Carol, bless her heart, had the "C" word diagnosed in both of her breasts. I must say she has been a trooper about the whole affair.

I was at the hospital for the biopsy and later flew to Chicago for a speaker's meeting. My sister was on my mind so much and I wanted to cheer her up. Miraculously, Steadman, Oprah's boyfriend, walk into one of the meetings. I had an idea. I introduced myself and asked him if he would please talk with my sister to give her a boost. Steadman graciously consented. I phoned my sister and they had such a nice chat! She was so excited about her call that she told all of her friends. No one believed her.

Carol is a bit obsessed over the reconstruction process. Just the other day we were at a funeral standing around in the churchyard waiting for the minister to start the burial service. This was the first time Carol was officially out in public since her surgery. It was rather chilly that day so she wore her faux mink vest under her coat. A cousin of mine stroked her mink vest, and whispered, "Kitty, kitty." "Yeah," Carol whispered casually, "I had them removed a few weeks ago."

I was speaking in Winchester, Virginia around Valentine's Day and I mentioned to the audience that it warms a wife's heart to be given fancy lingerie. After the program a sweet young woman approached me and commented how glad she was I had made that suggestion. "My husband only buys me them 'Hanes Her Way' drawers that come up real high. They is nice drawers and got the cotton crotch but I sure would like some of them fancy high-cut drawers. The only thing I got in my house that is French-cut is my green beans."

Greatest Success Principle in the Universe

Just think of any person who has ever achieved success in their lives and this will hold true. This one word if properly instituted can make the difference between absolute success and total failure. Are you ready? Here it is…the word is *recovery* or, in this case, just fake it. So simple. Are you able to do it? My friend, Susan James taught me all about recovery.

During pageant week, Susan, or Miss Hampton-Varnville, knew she was resting on the line of the "top ten list." The "top tenners" are the young ladies with the highest scores who will proceed on Saturday night to compete for the crown. If it helped these gals would pluck the rhinestones out of their crowns with their teeth.

The big announcement is made at the beginning of the Saturday night telecast for the final performances in swimsuit, evening gown and talent—all in front of a six-state audience.

Susan was ready. I watched her from the Observer Section (next year's wannabe-queen sitting area) perform a foot stompin' tap dance routine and show-off her perfect legs in swimsuit complete with her dazzling smile. Now all that was left was evening gown competition.

I watched her during rehearsal on Friday walk down a long flight of carpeted stairs—her footing was impeccable. I studied her every move as she floated with grace and confidence to the microphone. I listened as she recited her evening gown speech knowing the countless hours she had practiced looking in a mirror. Her head swiveled like an oscillating fan as she made perfect eye contact with the audience and judges. She was good. Still, Susan confided in me that she needed "a little something extra" to help push her into the top ten category.

I will never forget how Susan looked as she stood at the top of the staircase that evening. She was radiant in her Stephen Yearick designer gown and Cinderella slippers. It was her moment to charm the judges and seal her fate for the rest of the evening. What happened next made Susan James a household pageant icon even until this day.

She took her first step and the heel of her shoe got stuck in the hem of her gown. She completely missed the next three steps and tumbled down in an out-of-body experience. The audience was aghast. The next year's wannabe-queen section was as out of control as Susan's helpless body parts. We grabbed each other like a flock of scared biddies—some cackled and others squawked as Susan made her untimely descent. It was nothing short of a miracle when Susan somehow, thank you Jesus, got her footing at the bottom of those slick, carpeted stairs.

With the audiences' lingering expressions of horror and the mumbling of conversation, Susan approached the microphone. She stopped. She stared into the vastness of the universe and stood. My heart ached, "Oh, no! She has forgotten her speech!!!!" And right there at the Greenville Memorial Auditorium on that hot, July night, a beautiful girl in a twisted designer gown simply said. *"Well, I had some trip down here."* First silence, then a gradual roar of applause and cheering. The kind where you want to hoist someone up on your shoulders and carry them around the room. Oh, yes, Ma'am. It did seal her fate. She made the "Top Ten."

I could not tell you who won the preliminaries that Friday night, but I will never forget Susan James, Miss Hampton-Varnville, The Queen of Recovery.

Eleanor and Benjamin—my two biggest fans

My official Miss
South Carolina photo

CHAPTER 4

Fat Girlfriends, Skinny Girlfriends, and Crazy Girlfriends

All of my girlfriends are "fat." My mother is a fat girlfriend. In fact, I consider myself a fat girlfriend.

These are females in your life who love you unconditionally. They should be considered some of your greatest blessings. They are happy for you when things go well and cry with you when crummy stuff happens. They tell you the truth and expect the same in return.

On the other hand, beware of skinny girlfriends—they are your competition. No matter how much they pretend to like you, your sole purpose in life is to make them look good. They will cut you.

Love-Your-Hair-Hope-You-Win!

This skinny girlfriend thing played out before my very eyes at a small town pageant. The reigning queen was tacky, no doubt about it. You could just guess that about a year ago on Miss America night she was with her boyfriend sitting in his trailer watching the pageant. Around the first commercial he probably said something like, "Darlene, you is twice as purty as them girls. I bet you could whoop-up on them queens and win Miss 'Uhmerika! Why don't you git a purty dress and show them people a thing or two!"

Of course this led to her winning the local title because of her clogging routine to the country music classic, "Drop Kick me Jesus Through the Goal Post of Life." And since there were only three contestants, she also won swimsuit. But alas the state pageant was not kind to her so the boyfriend decided everything was rigged. After she gives up the crown, they will get married. I bet her crown will be woven with netting and serve a dual purpose as another head ornament on her wedding day.

So the tacky queen talked her "best" friend, who will be her maid of honor, into being in the pageant. Well, the friend was right attractive. I was impressed with her sense of style. She had that Jackie "O" look. At dress rehearsal her evening gown was white, one-shouldered, slit up the left leg and fit her like a glove. I thought this girl could easily be the winner.

After rehearsal I overheard the conversation that would be the death of her winning. "Girl, we need to sparkle that dress! Let's you and me add some sparkly stuff to your gown." I did not pay much attention until the next night when the curtain opened for evening gown competition. That tacky reigning queen talked her friend into putting glue glitter, that's right, multi-colored glue glitter all over that gown. You learn in kindergarten that glue makes things get smaller!

I'm telling you that girl struggled to walk. The top of the slit in that dress was now resting atop her hip. You could not even tell the dress was "one-shouldered." She had to stop before she stepped up on the ramp and turn sideways walking like a Blue-Tip Crab. The whole time on stage she made a face like she was praying that dress would not rip in two. The only people that enjoyed their view were the WASPS (White Anglo-Saxon Protestants) males who were part of the judges panel.

That so-called queen friend of hers knew better than to glitter that dress with glue. You could tell after the pageant when she went up to her crying she did not mean it. She was just sad that she was not the queen anymore.

People like this, it's all about them past, present and future. I don't care how old or what sex they are. This is a case of "the skinny girlfriend." I have learned to stay away from them as far as east is from west. My hope is that I live long enough to see them pork-up and ride through Walmart in one of those electric-shopping carts.

How do you drown a beauty queen?
Put a mirror in the bottom of a swimming pool.

Crazy Girlfriends

By far the best girlfriends are "fat girlfriends " who are also crazy. They are the ones who talk you into doing ridiculous things and never change with the passage of time. Crazy girlfriends remind us to lighten up and just have fun.

Candi is one of my best girlfriends who is a kick in the pants. My introduction to Candi was detecting a strong Minnesota Yankee accent (she was christened a Southerner shortly after) echoing down the hall on third floor my freshman year in college. Everyone fell in love with this homesick Yankee with a heart the size of Lake Superior. Through the years, Candi and I had adventures that were so crazy they could not be made up.

Candi and I got married about the same time. We sent her a lovely gift and never heard back (she almost lost her status as an honorary Southern Belle). Finally after several months we got a thank you. As I opened the note, her wedding picture floated gracefully to the floor. The note read, "Hey you guys! Well, I got a divorce but I love the gift!" I called her and asked when she decided she had made a mistake. She replied, "Well, Janie, I woke up the first day of my honeymoon and looked at him and said, 'You know, I think I made a mistake.'"

Twenty plus years later I visited Candi on the eve of wedding number two. Her husband-to-be invited us over for dinner. Not only is he a fabulous cook, he also enjoys cleaning. In short, Candi was marrying a wife. I have always wanted a wife and I know I will never have a wife. It took her 20 plus years but she got a wife out of the whole deal. God knew what he was doing. To say Candi is domestically challenged is a massive understatement.

On one of my trips to Minnesota, my buddy Lisa, accompanied me. Candi informed us that she was on a diet. Well, for two days we drank coffee and shook. Can you imagine? At breakfast we had a cup of coffee. Followed by the same menu for lunch and dinner. All of this while her two Schnauzers dined on Kibbles and Bits. On day two those dog biscuits were looking pretty good to me.

And speaking of the dogs, Candi tried to convince me that her dogs are really people. She would ask all the time, "Don't you think they understand and are really people? I mean what do you see when you look at them?" My answer was pretty simple, "Dogs." She wanted me to say "people" but I just would not say it.

Have mercy, she loved those dogs! She made plans for them to wear little outfits to walk down the aisle in her wedding.

One night we were watching the movie, *Cape Fear*. Scared to death we (dogs included) were huddled in Candi's double bed. I was so terrified I accidentally kicked one of her dogs on the floor. Well, she made me move to the floor and the dog was given my spot on the bed. The reason she made me move to the dog-bed was because I did not think her dogs were people.

Well, back to the second romance, more specifically Candi's second wedding. It was for family only so I was not invited. I could not wait to get the details. Finally the call came and yes, it was vintage Candi just like I expected. It seems that she had forgotten all about music for her walk down the aisle. Candi noticed the awkwardness of the moment as she began her descent down a stairway to the altar. As if it had been intentionally done, her mother, Mickey, started the familiar wedding march chanting—dum-dum-da-dum, dum, dum-da-dum...and so on. Candi said suddenly the entire congregation joined-in singing along with Mickey. It was a moment.

Candi is a classic example of a principle rule of being a queen—don't sweat (or if you are from the South the word is, mist) the small stuff.

Official Miss America
Wannabe photo

Bare foot Johns Island
farm girl goes to the
Miss America Pageant

CHAPTER 5

If Your Mouth Was a River, You Would Drown Yourself

Well, Tell Me About Yourself

I t's all about communication. This is one aspect that won't develop wrinkles, chemically dependent hair, or sag with age. Our communication skills improve as time passes.

Call it whatever, interview is where I learned the fine art of expression. There are two kinds of skills: dumb and smart. Here is dumb.

At the Coastal Carolina Fair I was a contestant vying for the title of the "Coastal Carolina Fair Queen." The semi-finalists were announced and all seven of us stood together, holding hands, waiting for the slaughter. The first on-stage question went to a cute, little, blonde Barbie. She was scared to death. The emcee simply asked, "How do you feel about the rate of crime?" Poor thing was totally confused and asked to hear the question again. After a very pregnant pause she replied, "I am sorry, I don't know anything about meat." It's hard to clap when somebody says something that stupid. She thought the question was "How do you feel about the rate of PRIME?"

I love interview, but there have been many times I have thought, "Girl, where is your brain!" Sitting in the interview a few years ago, a girl was asked, "How do you feel about euthanasia?" To which she replied, "I feel so sorry for them young people in Asia." Try sitting for the next eight minutes with a straight face after hearing that answer.

Another classic interview "faux pas" was when I asked a contestant if she had any special skills. "Yes!" she answered enthusiastically, "I can write with my left and right hands. I am amphibious."

At one pageant a friend of mine asked, "What kind of person do you enjoy associating with?" Her answer was simply, "People who have had hardships in life. I have a friend who is paralyzed from the waist down. He is a paraphernalia."

Pageant Answers: Then and Now

Funny how our answers change over the years. In fact, all of our answers change with maturity and the passage of time.

Question: *Jane, if you could be anyone else for 24 hours, who would you be and why?*

Answer: (Jane then) *I would like to be the First Lady of the United States so I could help other people.* (Jane now) *I would like to be a State Trooper, drive a Camero and give traffic tickets to people who get on my nerves.*

Question: *Jane, if you could invent something to help people, what would it be?*

Answer: (Jane then) *It would be a way we could all love each other and live in perfect harmony.* (Jane now) *I would invent a self-cleaning refrigerator.*

Question: *What is the most impressive thing you have ever done?*

Answer: (Jane then) *I traveled to Europe and studied The National Health Care System.* (Jane now) *I changed a diaper, vacuumed the floor, and rolled my hair all at the same time.*

Question: *Jane, describe the perfect man.*

Answer: (Jane then) *The perfect man is witty, considerate and supportive.* (Jane now) *The perfect man would have a "switch" so I could change him according to my needs. If I had use for him to be a romantic stud, I would turn the switch one way. But if I needed my hair and nails done, I would turn the switch the other way.*

Question: *What is your dream car?*

Answer: (Jane then) *A Porche with leather interior and a Bose Stereo system.* (Jane now) *A Suburban with Michelin tires.*

Question: *After the pageant what will you be searching for?*

Answer: (Jane then) *A husband.* (Jane now) *I need a wife.*

"There is only one thing we can do better than anyone else; we can be ourselves."
– William Ward Arthur

"Come on! Open your mouth and sound off at the sky!
Shout loud at the top of your voice,
I AM I!
ME! I am I!
And I may not know why
But I may know that I like it.
Three cheers! I AM I!"

– Dr. Seuss, *Happy Birthday to You!*

CHAPTER 6

To Get What You Want Act Like You Already Got It

How Big Is Your Fight?

When I was working for Allis Chalmers Tractor Company, I had the opportunity to travel throughout the Southeast performing for trade shows and in dealerships promoting equipment. It was a wonderful job and I loved meeting all of the different folks.

One night in South Georgia, I noticed the marquee at our hotel advertising, "Female Mud Wrestling." Well, I could not resist! I talked my traveling companion into going.

In the center of a big barroom was a huge pit filled with black mud. Amid cheers and thunderous applause, two women were introduced who would battle it out. The winner would receive $200.00.

The first contestant weighed in at 120 lbs. soaking wet. I knew she was in big trouble when "Big Mama" was introduced. She must have weighed in at 250 lbs. dehydrated! We all knew it was just a matter of time after the bell rang.

What a shock to all when Big Mama was pinned face down in that pile of mud! It made no sense until I remembered the quote, *"It is not the size of the dog in the fight but the size of the fight in the dog."*

Run Little Piggy!

We have a pig in our small, peaceful community of "Harmony" that is a pest. Ironically, this pig is making our community everything but harmonious. The pig came out of nowhere and has been living in our yards for a month or so. It rotates from home to home; I guess you could say it is a homeless pig.

The other day my mother-in-law, who is a kind and gentle person, threw a rock at it. Twice it has been hit by a car and reported dead, but the pig is still alive.

Later, we found out the pig belongs to a farm worker named Hamp. Unfortunately he is unable to catch it due to a strange accident. It seems he was intoxicated and sat on a hot, kerosene heater thinking it was the toilet. That just hurts even to think about.

These days, the pig has taken temporary residency in Aunt Naomi's yard. So now it has become Aunt Naomi's pig. Aunt Naomi is not at all happy to have a pig live in her yard. But Aunt Naomi's dogs are nice to the pig, so it feels like it belongs.

The reason this interests me is Aunt Naomi's dogs run after her car. They are all at church when she is at church and anywhere else Aunt Naomi goes. It has been many years since I moved here, and for all of those years, Aunt Naomi's dogs have always followed her around the community, running after her car.

Just the other day I saw Aunt Naomi's car, the dogs running in random order, and in last place, the pig. It was visibly in pain, panting and sweating...reminds me of that fat boy in second grade. Bless its heart. It was trying to keep up with the rest of the crowd; it wants to be like them.

To Get What You Want Act Like You Already Got It

I thought of the quote, *"If you can't run with the big dogs, stay on the porch."* Well, not this pig. I have to say I admire this pig for even trying.

How many times do we feel as if we have to wait until everything is perfect before we try something different? I have learned that the quicker you try something new, the quicker you learn if it works or not. Best of all we can learn productive lessons. Why not try to run with the big dogs...you may surprise yourself.

53

On the Boardwalk
in Atlantic City

Genuine Southern Belles of the real South

CHAPTER 7

Vote for Yourself

At the Flowertown Festival in Summerville, South Carolina, we were asked to vote for Miss Congeniality. I won by one vote; I voted for myself and asked Miss Lexington to vote for me.

I heard in one pageant there were 20 contestants and the vote for Miss Congeniality was a 20-way tie. The contestants had to vote again; this time for **two** girls they wanted to be Miss Congeniality. After the second vote, they had a winner.

The Naked Chicken

When I worked for Allis Chalmers Tractor Company, I rode down many long interstates with mile after mile of nothing. One day I noticed a chicken truck loaded with broilers on its way to becoming grocery store items. Feathers where flying down the interstate behind the speeding truck—nothing unusual. As we made our approach I noticed something on the top of a cage. I fixed my eyes on this object until we were on the side of the speeding semi. It was a chicken. Not only had it escaped from its cage but it was featherless—completely naked. The chicken was holding on to the top of the truck with every fiber in its little pink body. I knew the odds were against it but I was pulling for the thing. The truck would lag behind as it traveled up grades of highway then pass us on the way down. This continued for at least 40 miles. I was fascinated watching that chicken hang on. The forces of wind may have weighed on my "interstate entertainment"; eventually it may have "gone with the wind." I don't know. The last time the truck zoomed by, the chicken was still on its mission.

Today when I go to the poultry section at BiLo, I think about that chicken. It reminds me of the price we pay for holding on to something we believe in. First, we have to believe in ourselves enough to get out of "the cage." Voting for yourself is the first step to being free.

CHAPTER 8

Fixin' Up

Hair-do's and Fingernails

For a queen to look her best she knows that it is a three-fold process: physical, mental and emotional. You don't have to shop at the most expensive boutiques (although I love to shop at those places) and you don't have to jet out to Hollywood for the latest and greatest beauty secrets. Hey, you don't have to look like Barbie! I have known large women who look fabulous. Just like being a queen is all attitude so is looking like a queen. Adopt good, common sense, grooming principles and you can look like you just stepped off the runway.

My mother taught me this lesson early. She always looks wonderful. In the morning she dresses, puts on make-up and then appears. My mother is perfectly groomed.

My sister and mother shared a "2 X 4" room on an Alaskan Cruise for seven days. Not once did my sister see my mother without makeup.

As a child I would sit in wonder and watch my mother paint her nails Fire Engine Red. Yes, Eleanor has some claws. Even when times on the farm were hard Eleanor was always stylish—right down to her toes.

Speaking of toes, I would be remiss not to mention Eleanor's. They were also painted red and should have been registered weapons with the Federal Government. As children if we ever "cut a shine" Eleanor used her toes to inflict pain. She could literally transform her toes into pliers. When her toes made contact with your skin—watch out!

Many crabs have pinched me but nothing compares to the pain Eleanor can inflict with those toes of hers. Your skin would be red for days if her toes made contact. They are legendary.

We all celebrate that one special day of the week. Regardless of bad weather, car trouble or sickness, this day is honored at the same time at the same place. It matters not what is going on in the world. Every Southern woman with good sense knows what special day I am referring to—hair day.

Women are transformed into queens this day. Fridays are big hair days in the South. Southern Baptist women want good hair for Sunday. Working Southern Baptists go to the beauty shop on Saturdays.

I watch them enter their respected beauty shops, shoulders slumped and heads down. Only a few hours later, the beauty shop door opens to reveal a new creation.

And all of us "churin" knew and still know that nothing will interfere with Thursday that was once Wednesday. My daddy frequently commented that he hoped he would not die and mess up Momma's hair day. Bless his heart, it's like his body just knew the right day of the week to pass.

My mother was hospitalized and had open-heart surgery. It is worth noting that according to the Intensive Care Staff at Roper Hospital my mother is the only woman to have her hair "fluffed" in the Intensive Care Unit. My sister and I prayed for God to give us a sign that Momma would get well. He did.

Even "the sistas" who work in the cafeteria at the hospital have a special time when they get their nails and hair "did." Their hair-dos are nothing short of works of art. My sister and I fell in love with "the sistas." We patronized the café at least four times a day to get their world famous chicken salad sandwiches. They always asked about Momma and helped us through some tough days.

For a true queen to look good has nothing to do with money. I've seen wealthy women wear the wrong clothes and look like a tired sack of potatoes. Good posture is essential. Just fill those lungs with air, walk with your head up and wear a pleasant expression. Wear clothing that complements you and your lifestyle.

Good grooming does not equal loads of make-up. I always thought Tammy Bakker uglied herself with all of that horrible mascara and lipstick. Be natural. Use some color that, once again, complements you and your lifestyle.

It is fun to walk into a department store and see the "make-up babes" at their respected cosmetic counters. Yeah, I want to look like a clown.

One time the reigning "Miss World" fixed my hair and makeup. When she was finished I looked just like her. My mother burst out laughing when she saw me.

And, oh, please, update! I had my picture made with a man who shoots all the Miss America contestants. At the time I was still holding on to my beauty queen big hair. I walked into his studio, he took one look at me and he asked, "So are you a speaker or an old beauty queen?" I did not know this man from Adam and I shocked myself by saying, "Cut it." And cut he did. He changed my looks so much until people did not recognize me! Even my children did not know who I was.

All the women loved the new look but, of course, the men said, "Oh, why did you cut your hair?" Men love long hair. Even if it looks like rats played in it, they still love long hair. The only man I know who admits loving short, sassy hair is my jeweler, Danny. Not only does he love short hair he lets me charge jewelry. (After all, I am not waiting until I am old and wrinkled so show off my jewelry. Get it while your skin has elasticity.)

CHAPTER 9

Flaming, Bladed Batons

You don't have to sing like Beverly Sills or color co-ordinate like Martha Stewart. Just be really good at something that makes you like yourself. In other words…have a talent!

Rhinestones on a Cow Pie

You can always tell when a contestant is twirling flaming, bladed batons…one only has to observe the audience. There is a look of frozen horror fixed on the faces of the masses. Call it what you will but in the South we call it *talent*.

In a rural, Illinois community a group of leaders decided they needed a queen. So, in an attempt to copy our graceful Southern ways, a pageant was proposed. Notice was sent to the area schools and an eager group of young ladies assembled.

Several questions concerning talent were asked. The response of "do what you do best" was advised to the wannabe-beauty queens. Well, it just so happened that one particular "wannabe" held another title: "The 4-H Cow Milking Champion." And don't you know, this young lady, not having just fallen off the cattle truck, was no dummy and checked out the Miss America rulebook. And nowhere in that book did it mention "no live animals on stage." At the time there was no such rule but honey, today it is in that rulebook as big as you please in bold print. I guess you have made the connection by now this is the very event that created the rule that forever changed the lives of beauty queens across America.

Dress rehearsal, Friday night. Our contestant drives up to the auditorium transporting a big ol' "has-not-been-milked-all-day" Holstein, in other words, her talent. This creates quite a stir with the pageant committee since her application stated her talent is a "classical musical rendition of the Viennese Waltz." Yes Sirre, this gal not only had culture but even a little agriculture in mind.

With her three-legged stool, positioned to grip her "instruments," and bucket underneath the soundman played their song. Yes, she commenced to milk that cow to the tune of the Viennese Waltz. Now y'all, I ain't makin' this up.

Hitting the sides of that galvanized bucket rivaled the magnificent works of Mozart himself. It went something like this…Du, Du, Du, du-du-squirt, squirt, squirt, squirt. Du, Du, Du, du-du-squirt, squirt, squirt, squirt….you get the picture.

The rulebook was grabbed as the committee tried to convince our girl that she could not in any way perform with a live animal on stage. Sitting there in complete confidence this girl knew her stuff. So prepared was she. There was a much larger bucket present to aid with any full bladder or other unspeakable problems. After the proverbial "what-ifs" were exchanged, the committee knew there was no stopping her.

The curtain opened that next evening with the bevy of beauties doing their thing. The pageant progressed flawlessly and then, the moment those "in the know" dreaded most, approached. The audience gasped as the curtain was drawn to reveal what would turn out to be the most memorable performance in the history of pageant competition.

The music began and our girl, as poised as any Miss America has ever been, played her "utterly fabulous" cow. The crowd sat motionless soaking in the magical moment. One small handclap quickly escalated into a thunderous roar of applause. The bliss of the moment was short-lived. The cow let out a "moo" that shook the building to its foundation. "Red flags" waved, as did the cow's tail.

Those of you who are not from a farm background may think the cow was applauding, too. Our contestant knew better as did a member of the pageant committee. Both contestant and committee member raced to the same place at the same time in an attempt to fetch the BIG bucket. But, alas, the cow beat 'em to the punch. Time for that phrase we all know and love; when you gotta go, you gotta go. And go this cow did.

In an attempt to grab the BIG bucket, the contestant and committee member tripped over the main power cord and unplugged the lights, sound, etc. In a darkened building the only sounds heard were the mooing of the relived animal and well, the other.

During the next several minutes of complete bedlam, the building was evacuated and the cow was removed from the stage as was the "cow-wee."

What happened next is the point of the entire story. That darlin', little ol', honorary, Southern Belle only had one question. Still poised she walked up to the pageant committee and asked, "Can I do it again?"

This is one of the finest queen's rule and colossal success principle—don't ever stop trying.

Every time I share this story someone will ask—"Did she win"? Did she win! DID SHE WIN! Well, she won the best title of all—the girl who got rid of beauty queen animal tricks.

However, the biggest prize was her attitude of giving it another try or squirt, if you will.

And I have a feeling today that she just may be the first female president of the National Dairy Association. Hopefully she will read this story and hire me to speak at her next convention.

CHAPTER 10

That Dog Won't Hunt, Point, or Even Get off the Porch

If you really want to fail at something, do what I did.

Pink Cadillac

I sold Mary Kay for a while. I love the idea of working as a consultant because you can work out of your home, try to be a good mother and make some money. I was no good at it. I was not using my God-given gifts. ***You will never be fulfilled if you are not using your gifts***. I became something I should not have been, a Mary Kay consultant.

I went to my first rally and everybody was clapping and cheering. All of these "pink-ladies" were passionate about makeup, all of them except me. I just could not bring myself to clap and cheer over a tube of lip-gloss. I was not convinced the makeup agreed with my skin. I knew I needed to be able to wear it and love it. This was mistake number two; ***don't ever sell or do anything you do not totally believe in***.

I got just enough motivation from that meeting to schedule my very first Mary Kay party. It was a miracle! The phone rang the next day and my inaugural party was booked. I told the hostess-to-be the Mary Kay rules—have the party in a cool room with some refreshments on hand, etc.

I was all dressed up with my Mary Kay smile and all-important pink bag loaded with everything a face could desire: cleanser, exfoliater, moisturizer, concealer, base make-up, eye shadow, lip color and lip gloss. I was ready!

Upon arriving at the house, red flags popped-up immediately. First the house was located in a not-so-good section of town. And remember that "cool" room that the party was to be in? Well, it was hotter that Phoenix in August. My makeup melted right off my face. In the "cool" room were the following appliances: a refrigerator, hot water heater, freezer, dryer, washing machine…just pick any appliance, it was in that room emitting heat. The majority of the guests were 18 and under with the exception of the grandmother. Remember the refreshments? They were covered with flies. All I could think of was my Grandmother McElveen saying, "Every time a fly lands it lays an egg."

To make matters worse, there was an old drunken grandfather in the next room watching television. One time he yelled, "Hit don't matter how much that paint y'all put on yo face, y'all is still gonna be ugly. You can't fix ugly."

To add to the tragedy in progress, there was a little boy there who ran up to me and grinned from ear to ear. He was cute until I studied his mouth. The child had no teeth, only pieces of skin hanging! I just blurted out, "What happened to his teeth!?" The grandmother said, "Well, he sucked the bottle too long. He ain't never gotten teeth." Finally, the grandfather and little boy left the house. One less thing to worry about. After all, the Mary Kay show must go on.

I proceeded to follow the rules flawlessly. I loaded the pink trays with all the latest Mary Kay colors and described each one in detail. We cleansed, we exfoliated, we moisturized and finally it was time for the highlight of the show—applying makeup.

"Okay, Ladies," I said. "This is the eye make-up! Let's apply this to our eyelids." Suddenly, there was a chorus of "oohs" and "ahas" concerning the grandmother's lovely eye color. Well, the grandmother got a little carried away and put lipstick on her eyelids.

Just then the screen door slammed and the grandfather and little boy appeared. The toothless child ran up to me and grinned from ear to ear. Each "nub" was decorated with one of those chocolate candy "footballs."

At the end of the show I sold a tube of lip-gloss and quit the business.

I love a parade!

Me and my
Mr. America

CHAPTER 11

Red, Ripe Tomatoes and the Eiffel Tower

It's hard to believe that leaning over picking tomatoes in a hot, Johns Island, tomato field eventually got me to the top of the Eiffel Tower. A long journey made simple by five principles—truths I must share.

This chapter will not make you laugh; it will make you think. Chuckles will be placed with a vine ripe, staked, irrigated, un-culled harvest of down-home wisdom.

My journey to the top of the Eiffel Tower began in my own backyard. I started a wholesale tomato business that helped me earn money for college in addition to teaching timeless success principles. The long, hot hours I spent working in my Daddy's tomato fields still have an impact on my life.

Hard Work

Early in the morning, I would drag myself out of bed to fill my tomato orders. One of the most important things to do was, beat the heat. As soon as the dew was dry on the tomato stems, I would pick as many tomatoes as possible. To fill the remaining orders I would crawl around in 1,000 lb. wooden crates and rescue the tomatoes that would be culled at the shed.

Whether I was working on the truck or in the field itself, the work was hard. I mentally prepared myself for a long day of hot, demanding work.

Go the Extra Mile

After my orders were filled, I would take the tomatoes home and wash off all of the fertilizer. This made the fruit look shiny and delicious. I did not have to go to all that trouble, but I discovered folks appreciate attention to detail.

Be Consistent

As I delivered my orders, there was one man who was hard to please. I thought if I put the best tomatoes on top he would buy the boxes. Did he surprise me! He did not care what the tomatoes looked like on the top; he wanted to see the last tomato on the very bottom.

Just like that bucket of tomatoes, people stay successful when they are consistent with their personal and professional lives.

Show People What They Want

There was a produce man who represented a large grocery store who never ordered a single tomato from me! After repeatedly calling him, I paid him a visit. "Mr. Jones, I just want you to see what you have been missing," I said with a sweet grin. With that comment, I showed him the biggest tomatoes I could find in the field. "I'll take 150 lbs.!" he exclaimed.

I showed him what he wanted. Did he need those tomatoes? No, but he did want them. Need equals desperation. Want is a powerful force because it is connected with emotion.

Remember How You Got There

I worked so hard over the past few years in the tomato fields, Daddy decided to reward me with the chance to study music and art in Europe for six weeks. Towards the end of my trip, I was in Paris standing on the top of the Eiffel Tower in awe of the view. I remember commenting, "Well, I am standing on the top of the Eiffel Tower, but one week from today, I will be leaning over picking tomatoes."

I was right. I was not too proud to go back to those hot tomato fields. After all, that job got me to the top of the Eiffel Tower, on the Dean's List in College, down a runway of the Miss America Pageant, and the list goes on....

My first album cover...
Light the Light

Easter Sunday with
my sweet babies

CHAPTER 12

Find the Funny

*"Nancy Reagan and I have a lot in common.
We both love our husbands, we both have our
charities, Nancy wears a size 4 and so does my leg."*
— **Barbara Bush**

I learned quickly to find the humor in life and pageants are loaded with lessons in laughter.

Roses, Mermaids, Apples, Peaches, etc....

Every weekend queens from every intersection or crossroad in South Carolina were invited to compete for various titles across the state: the South Carolina Peach Queen, Sea Island Mermaid, Queen of the Carolina Sea Islands, Miss Grape, Apple Queen, Rose Queen, Watermelon Queen, and Miss Southern 500. A girl could win money to help offset the expenses of being in the Miss South Carolina Pageant.

At the South Carolina Peach Festival, the town had not had a festival in 25 years. To commemorate the event, the festival committee cooked the largest peach pie in the world. All of the queens had the honor of being the first to taste it. The problem was the pie was completely cooked but the health department would not let the cooks turn off the oven. So the festival committee was forced to continue cooking an already done pie. With TV cameras rolling from Charlotte, Greenville, and Spartanburg, the wannabe-peach-queens were all given a generous serving of this black liquid with something that resembled a peach floating in it. All of us at the same time tasted it and spit it out. Except one girl who said it was delicious. She knew about the "peach pie tragedy" and topped her "pie" with mounds of vanilla ice cream. She won the pageant.

At the Beaufort Water Festival, I was shocked to be announced in the "top seven" for the title of Sea Island Mermaid. This was the swimsuit portion of the pageant. My best buddy, Miss Greenwood, was ticked-off that I made the cut and she did not. As I walked on stage, she poked-in the cups of my swimsuit so I had two big dents on each side. I looked like the Concave Queen. Needless to say, I did not win.

It was in this particular pageant that I learned the fine art of wearing false eyelashes. Rule number one, don't wear them in an outdoor pageant on the coast where the wind is blowing. During collective judging, I felt my eyelash pulling loose and eventually it blew off. On the command, "quarter turn to the right, ladies," I saw my eyelash, stuck in Miss Myrtle Beach's hair.

A truly memorable moment took place at the South Carolina Rose Festival. Picture this, beauty queens walking gracefully through the lovely rose gardens putting on their best performances for the judges. All of a sudden a huge snake falls out of an oak tree and lands on one of the contestants. We screamed, kicked-off our spiked-heel shoes, and ran like a bunch of schoolgirls. So much for poise.

My least favorite festival pageant was Miss Southern 500. The day before the actual pageant we had to go to the racetrack and meet some very "important" people. They asked us to wear "hot pants" which, by the way, were not in style. They would provide T-shirts for us. (I was not surprised when they were size "Barbie.") Picture this: white hot pants, extra small T-shirts and white high heel shoes—right in line with the Miss America image.

We were supposed to have our T-shirts signed by these "important people." All of a sudden this guy behind me asked, "Hey, Darlin', want me to sign yer T-shirt?" I sarcastically replied, "Only if I can sign yours." So, we exchanged signatures. I thought the whole incident was a joke and put the T-shirt away somewhere.

Fifteen years later, while shopping at BI-LO, I saw on a box of Tide the autograph of the man who signed my T-shirt. Where did I put that Ricky Rudd shirt? I wonder if he still has my signature?

After being crowned Miss South Carolina I found myself on the super highway of preparing for the Miss America Pageant. Monday morning after winning the pageant, I was sitting in a beauty shop by Miss Walhalla's grandmother. Not knowing who I was, she began to tell me how the new Miss South Carolina was ugly and could not sing. I just sat there and agreed with her.

"Sometimes a laugh is the only weapon we have."
– Roger Rabbit

Pulled to Reality

The Christmas season was in full swing and for beauty queens this means endless parades. I was on top of the world; ride in a parade for 30 minutes, smile, wave and get paid $125.00.

In one day, I road in a purple sanitation truck, fire truck and walked BEHIND a team of Beef-a-Lo (combination of a cow and buffalo). It was hard to wave in that parade; I was more interested in where I was stepping or what I might step in.

That year of my life I vowed to never wear blue jeans or be seen without make-up. But, after the last Christmas parade, I hurried back to my apartment, took off my make-up, and put on an old pair of jeans to begin the long ride to my parents' home. I told myself it did not matter since no one would see me. Oh, was I wrong!

Not too far outside of Charleston, I heard the familiar sound of a siren whaling. I knew he had me. I was speeding.

"Driver's license, registration, please Ma'am." Chanted the patrolman as I scrambled in the glove compartment...I could see my face in his mirrored sunglasses. Talk about "plain Jane"! I knew I was in trouble when the officer took my driver's license and registration back to his car to write a ticket. What a shock when he handed me a "warning."

I was so excited, I handed him my official Miss South Carolina photograph; complete with gown, crown and loads of make-up. "Thank you so much," I said, "this is for you!" He looked at the picture, looked at me and then exclaimed, "Dog-gone! Do you know her?"

The Moth

Pageant season was in full swing, and I was asked to emcee the South Carolina Queen of Cotton Pageant in Bishopville, South Carolina. The pageant is in conjunction with the South Carolina Cotton Festival and, of course, the highlight of the festival is the crowing of Miss Cotton.

It seemed that I was making the rounds with the same panel of judges who were friends of mine. Before I was introduced the panel of my pageant friends mentioned in good-natured humor how sick they were of me telling the same story about the preacher and the bug. "Well, it's a great story," I said, "and perfect for this small town Southern Baptist crowd."

In a nutshell, this preacher had a knack for quoting scripture. The folks in his town were amazed at his ability to match Bible verses with particular situations. One hot, August day, the church had their revival service outside. Bugs were zooming everywhere. In the middle of a profound statement, while the preacher had his mouth WIDE open, a bug flew in. The congregation sat in suspense knowing there was no scripture to accommodate this situation. To everyone's surprise, the preacher took a deep breath, swallowed, and said, "A stranger came and I took him in!"

Before I knew it I was introduced, made my entrance and stood center stage. In front of me were huge footlights with moths the size of small airplanes fluttering about. I launched into my story. Right at the part where the bug flies into the preacher's mouth, one of those giant moths flew into my mouth! As I gasped for air, I felt the helpless creature struggling along with me. I pointed to my throat trying to get someone to give me some water. My pageant "friends" were laughing hysterically at me. To make matters worse, I realized that there was only one thing for me to do—swallow.

After the pageant was over, an older lady walked up to me laughing. "Honey, you was so funny. We was laughin' our heads off when you was actin' out that preacher."

I'm glad somebody enjoyed it.

Get Goin' With the Gleaner Combine

I was asked to emcee the Miss Anderson Pageant in Anderson, South Carolina. I had been traveling all week working for Allis Chalmers tractor company singing and promoting farm equipment. During my tractor shows I sang several songs about disk harrows, tractors and our number one seller: the Gleaner Combine. Also on the show tape was a wonderful medley of "You Needed Me" and "Let Me Be There." I discovered this medley served a dual purpose. I could also use it to entertain at pageants while the judges marked their final ballots.

Without thinking, I gave the soundman my show tape that had not been re-wound.

Well, the time came to ask for the judges' decision. The contestants were standing together, holding hands as the reigning queen took her final walk, cried and got flowers from her boyfriend or mother, etc. While this was going on I noticed the judges were still marking their ballots! I was not worried. I had my "old friend" medley standing by to use as a filler.

At the end of all of the farewells, the judges were still writing away!

I did what every experienced emcee does. I was ready for this moment; I was a pro. In fact, I love this moment. Excitement is high; you can almost hear a rhinestone drop. I milked it, "Yes, Ladies and Gentlemen, this is the highlight of our evening......the announcement of the new Miss Anderson! But all of our contestants are winners!!!! Let's hear it for them!"

Clap, clap, clap....."But, before I announce our runners-up and new Miss Anderson, I have a special song for the queens. It says everything about why we are here this evening. I would like to dedicate this next song to all of our contestants." I gracefully nodded to the soundman. Some contestants wiped their eyes, others sniffed. To my complete surprise, "Get Goin' With the Gleaner Combine" played instead of "You Needed Me." Well, what is an emcee to do? I sang the Gleaner Combine song.

The audience starred at me. The contestants were in semi-shock. The judges were frozen. No one really knew what to think. With the music still playing, I burst out laughing and explained what happened. Then everyone laughed.

Years later people still mention that pageant to me.

Can I Have Your Autograph?

I wish I had a penny for every time I was asked this question my year as Miss South Carolina. However, it is uncommon to hear this request after the crown is gone. I guess that is why it is so special if asked just one more time.

I was attending the Miss America Pageant at Convention Center in Atlantic City, New Jersey, for the second year in a row. This occasion was much more relaxing since I was officially an audience member and not a contestant. On Friday night I was seated in the Miss South Carolina box seats, mentally strolling down the runway. Dressed in sequins and feathers, I felt like a million dollars. Out of the corner of my eye, I spotted a young boy, his eyes fixed upon me. He was making his way to my side. Upon arrival he nervously stammered, "Can, can, I please have your autograph?" Astounded, I asked, "You mean you remember me?" "Oh, yes!" said the youngster. "You are my favorite queen. Everyone loves and remembers you!" I could actually feel the feathers on my gown puffing out to match the growing size of my head. With a grand sweep I took the Miss America program book from the young lad and with Hollywood flair, signed in large uppercase letters, my name and title. As I handed the program back to him, his eyes fell on the fresh ink. His face was the next to fall. He simply said, "You ain't Phyllis George?"

"A former beauty queen is about as popular as a cold plate of mashed potatoes."
– **Albert Marks, former president of the Miss America organization**

"Miss Jane, Is That You?"

If you haven't guessed already, pageants are a humbling experience. Even more so with the passage of time.

Caroline brought home her friend, Carli to spend the night. As Carli made her way through the entrance hall, she came to a screeching halt. "Miss Jane, who is that woman hanging on your wall?" she asked sweetly, referring to my pageant portrait. "Why that is my picture, Carli!" I said thinking the child must need glasses. "Miss Jane, did you have long hair?" she asked again. "Yes." I calmly answered. "Was that a long time ago?" Carli persisted. "YES, I guess so, Carli," I said losing my patience. Then she added the final blow, "IT MUST HAVE BEEN A MILLION YEARS AGO!"

"Time is fun when you are having flies."
– **Kermit the Frog**

Pretty Babies!

It's difficult for me to recall this next story without feeling a bit nauseous. A dear friend Jack Brantley, known for his fabulous foods and incredible Southern hospitality, roped Thomas and me into judging one of those delightful baby pageants. The categories began with "Newborn Miss," ages 0-6 months. I could not help but wonder how a baby age "0" was going to make its way to the platform. Were they planning on wheeling a gurney onto the stage with a mother in labor?

I soon discovered that adoring mothers lovingly paraded the newborns in front of the crowd. A chorus of "ooohs" and "aaah's" from the family members planted in the audience rippled throughout the room. My mind drifted to how I was going to get back at Jack.

"Okay, Ladies and Gentlemen, our first group of contestants is ready for individual competition," said the director/emcee. "Let's welcome our Tiny Baby Miss contestants!" Then the pageant director/emcee, so help me, said the unthinkable, "Our contestants will now begin swimsuit competition. Some of the mothers have taken the liberty of removing their diapers. So if these babies have 'accidents' on the stage, you judges don't count off."

"The bigger the hair
the smaller the town.
The bigger the crown
the smaller the pageant."
– Dale Smith Thomas, former Mrs. Tennessee

81

You Are One Fine Heifer!

I pride myself in being versatile, but I'll have to admit this self-acclaimed quality was put to the test a couple of years ago. My brother-in-law drove to our house one night and assembled the family to "share" some big news. "We are now owners of two stockyards!" My first thought was, well, good luck all you other people. Where I come from you "pet" animals, tie bows around their necks, and make up cute names for them.

Come to find out, I was drafted to work two days a week in the office adding, subtracting, and calculating bills. I could not help but remember the black Sharpie pen words written on my report cards, "must attend summer school in math." Great.

The first thing I noticed is the way some of the cattle buyers are shaped. From the back view they look like they live in Somalia. From a side view they look like the entire continent of Africa. Another thing I found out is whatever is in their heads comes out of their mouths unfiltered.

During my stockyard days, I desperately wanted to have a baby. It was getting to the sensitive stage; for example, a Pampers commercial would bring me to tears.

One day a buyer sat down by me and tried to carry on some sort of conversation. He said, "You got any chaps?" At first I thought he was asking if I wore those leather things over my pants. It dawned on me that he meant children. "No," I replied, with a quiver in my voice. "We want children but I have an ovulation disorder!" (Like he needed to know that.) He reared back in his seat and said, "Well, if you was my heifer and was not calving, I would have done drove you to the meat processin' plant." I lobed a good one right back at him. "If I were your heifer, I'd drive myself to the meat processin' plant."

"Honey, your speech was so funny
I gave you a standing ovulation!"
– "Compliment" shared after one of my speeches

Honey, Who Are You?

Many times people will ask me to share embarrassing moments during my tenure as Miss South Carolina. It does not take me long to recall my visit to the American Cancer Society Fashion Show.

That particular weekend, I remember being extremely tired. In addition to my regular appearances, I was also on the road with Allis Chalmers. I had been traveling all over the South that week and could not wait to get some r & r.

My host and hostess lived in a mansion. Seriously, their home was spectacular! This incredible house even had an observatory complete with a high-powered telescope so one could gaze at the stars. Well, the only stars I was interested in were in my dreams. I mentioned to my hostess who, by the way, was also emceeing the fashion show, that I was going to rest. She kept insisting that I make myself "at home," so I did. I decided to let my face "breathe" for a change, which translates to, not wearing any make-up. However, my hostess and I chatted face to face at length about the specifics of the show so we would both be on the same page. I was to appear on stage only twice, once in sportswear and the second time as a bride. She told me that I was the "star" of the show.

Late in the afternoon the day of the show, my hostess left to make sure all of the props and details were in place. I decided to put on my makeup for the first time since arriving and dress for the show.

The auditorium was packed. My mother drove from Charleston along with Thomas to see me make my grand appearance. I was standing in the wings all dressed up and ready to wow the audience. My hostess, now the emcee of the show, glanced at me and said, "Well, now let's welcome Judy!" I thought she was reading the wrong card so I did not move and waited for her to correct the mistake. "Sarah?" she said, with a strange lilt in her voice. "Are you Betty?" she inquired again. It finally dawned on me that she did not know who I was! With my ego shot down, I said, "I am, Jane." To which she asked, "Jane, who??" With my voice quivering I answered, "Jane Jenkins." Believe me, it got worse. "Oh, my goodness!" she exclaimed. "This is our guest of honor! Honey, I am sooooo sorry I did not recognize you with your makeup on. This is our own Miss South Carolina, but you should have seen her a few hours ago!" I could feel the heat coming off my face.

Let me share the rest of the story. Only last year I ran into that woman again. I introduced myself and recounted my visit in her home. She said, "I'm sorry. I have no idea who you are!" I wasn't surprised.

CHAPTER 13

High Heels to Bare Feet

Competing in the Miss American Pageant was my journey from bare feet to high heels. I believe the Miss America Program represents the finest young women mentally, physically and spiritually—everything I was told I was NOT but knew I could BECOME. I proved to myself that I could achieve something special.

My pageant days are memories I relive when I face new challenges in life. I remember walking down that long runway in Atlantic City when I stepped on the stage at Radio City Music Hall in front of a packed house. I told myself...*Jane if you can walk on that massive stage in Atlantic City, you can do this*. Just minutes earlier I was sitting in the Green Room with Charlton Heston while Colin Powell was speaking. It was such an honor to share the stage with these two men. Yes, Radio City Music Hall is a long way from the worn out stage on Murray Boulevard where it all started.

The point is what ever you do, do it well. Whoever you are, be the best person you can be. Take your own journey, but be able to return. Only in returning can you share what you learned with others. Don't let "who" you are be overpowered by "what" you become.

Carol, Tootsie, me and Wilhelmenia . . . The "Sista's"

Professional speaker
and singer or ...
an FBQ (Former
Beauty Queen)

CHAPTER 14

The Party's Over

It's a challenge to end a book. I've been avoiding writing this last story because it is so final. Words like: "finished, the end, last chapter, period," swim around in my head. So I thought I would end with a beginning.

All these stories about pageants.... I hope one does not think I am obsessed with beauty pageants. No, quite the contrary. I am passionate, though, about discovering how to be my personal best.

Here is the grand finale...the closing scene...the last song. In fact this story is about a song, the one I sang to win Miss South Carolina and my talent at the Miss America Pageant. This farewell was written and printed in the Miss South Carolina program book some twenty years ago. As I copy my words from an old, worn page the meaning is still fresh and new.

The Party's Over
It's time to call it a day
They've burst your pretty balloon and taken the moon away
It's time to wind up the masquerade…

Now you must wake up
All dreams must end
Take off your makeup…
The Party's Over
It's all over, my friend

My "party" began one year ago, but the preparations began long ago. I dedicated myself to something worth hours of disciplined thoughts and actions. So determined was I that my party was going to be different. No one was held responsible for the outcome, no one but Jane Louise Jenkins.

Like every party mine was full of unforgettable events: Miss America's Jubilee in Vicksburg, Mississippi; touring the South singing and promoting Allis Chalmers equipment; performing the National Anthem at the Hall of Fame Bowl; touring textile mills with the ambassador from China; traveling to Washington, DC for a reception with the congressional delegation from South Carolina; and mostly meeting Thomas Herlong, my former escort and future husband.

My party was celebrated with laughter, singing and much happiness. I enjoyed the wonderful gifts: a car, scholarship money, and new clothes! I must admit though, the greatest gifts were without a price. I received hearts full of endless love; friendships were unselfishly offered to me.

Certainly, no party is complete without a guest list. Everyday my list became longer because so many people were invited to share this special time in my life. One guest particularly stands apart from the rest because without Him none of this would have been possible. Through my Christian faith I learned the importance of being Miss South Carolina.

Quick, send in the clowns…the end is here. Well, I guess I'll have to sing a new song; my celebration continues.

My party's beginning
No, it's not over, my friends

Keep singing your song and celebrate your party…………

ACKNOWLEDGMENTS

To all my "fat girlfriends"...............

My fun, wonderful mother, Eleanor McElveen Jenkins, who gives me laughter and helped me become a person who can laugh.

My sister, Carol Jenkins Hardman, who is the bravest and funniest person I know.

My "Tootsie," Ruth Bligen, for being my second mother.

My barefoot buddy, Leize Glover Bennett, who understands it all.

My mother-in-law, Jewell Holmes Herlong, who is a "jewel."

Mary Holmes—who I want to become when (or if) I grow up.

My mentor, Dixie Culbreath—who tells me the truth.

Ginger Lynn—my sweet friend who laughs with me.

Sally Rauton—who makes me feel it is all right to not be all there.

Martha Herlong—for being my friend through it all.

Sandy Williams—for loving my children.

Genna Covar—for having children who are beautiful friends of my children.

Shirley Lott—for her heartfelt prayers and love.

Girlfriend family thanks: Dianne, Jo Anne, Sharon, Sue, Amy, Caroline, and precious Amy Patterson.

To all of the above for years of listening to me read these stories and asking for the billionth time, "Do you think this is funny?"

Special thanks to Connie Herlong and Jamie Bryson for helping me proofread.

In memory of three dear men that I miss every day:

- Robert H. Henry—you have been touched by the Master's hand.

- Charles Edward Holmes, the best Christian guy-friend in the universe.

- My sweet Daddy, Benjamin Roper Jenkins, who taught me the value of hard work and honesty.

Product Information

	Q⟍ᴛʏ	Aᴍᴏᴜɴᴛ
Bare Feet to High Heels		
Humorous book $10.00	____	_____
Yesterday and Today		
Cassette/CD Gospel Hymns $10.00	____	_____
Light the Light		
Cassette/CD Contemporary Christian		
Music $10.00	____	_____
You Decide!		
Cassette/CD Songs of motivation and		
inspiration $10.00	____	_____
The Magic of Being Yourself		
CD/Audio tape presentation $10.00	____	_____
Video tape presentation $20.00	____	_____
How to Be a VIP		
Youth presentation video $20.00	____	_____
Any three audiotapes for.................................... $25.00	____	_____
Purchase all tapes for ($80 value) $60.00	____	_____
Total package of tapes and Jane's book		
($90 value) $70.00	____	_____

Shipping & Handling US: $4 for the first item and $2 for each additional item.	Subtotal _____
	Sales Tax (6% for SC res.) _____
	Shipping / Handling _____
	TOTAL _____

Fax: (803) 275-2766 *(send this form or a copy of this form)*

Call: (803) 275-3388

Write: Jane Jenkins Herlong, 65 Bouknight Road, Johnston, SC 29832

Name: _____ Date: _____

Address: _____

City: _____ State: _____ Zip: _____

Phone: _____ Email _____

Payment type: ❑ Check / Money Order enclosed *(payable to: Jane Jenkins Herlong)*
❑ Credit card   ❑ Visa   ❑ Mastercard

Credit card #: _____

Name on card: _____ exp date: _____

Signature: _____